An accessi

C000212633

A collection of poetry, creative prose and other images celebrating the river Eden and its tributaries and the landscape surrounding them

Compiled by East Cumbria Countryside Project as part of Discover Eden

EAST CUMBRIA
couΠtryside
P R O J E C T

Published in 2007
East Cumbria Countryside Project
Warwick Mill, Warwick Bridge, Carlisle, Cumbria CA4 8RR

Cover illustration by Pip Hall

The quotation "from Mallerstang to the shifting Solway sands"
on the cover is a line from the November poem,
one of the twelve poems written by Meg Peacocke
for the Poetry Path at Kirkby Stephen

ISBN 978 1906244 14 9

Printed by Reeds Printers

CONTENTS

Landscape is not only seen with the eye, it is felt in the heart.

*From Heritage Lottery Fund guidance notes**

Cumbria's Garden of Eden

The river Eden rises above Mallerstang in the south eastern corner of Cumbria and flows north via Kirkby Stephen, Appleby, Temple Sowerby, Langwathby, Lazonby, Armathwaite, and Wetheral to Warwick Bridge where it turns west through Carlisle and out to sea beyond Rockcliffe and the Solway Firth - a distance of some 65 miles.

It is joined at regular intervals on its journey by a succession of tributaries, many of which are substantial rivers in themselves with their own sizeable tributaries. These include the Scandal, Swindale, Hoff, Lyvennet, Crowdundle, Lowther, Eamont, Raven, Irthing, Gelt, Petteril and Caldew, all emanating from hundreds of little becks flowing down from the surrounding hills and mountains.

The Eden catchment landscape covers an area of 2200 square kilometres and extends from the Lake District fells of Skiddaw and Helvellyn, and the two major lakes of Ullswater and Haweswater in the West, to the Scottish border in the North, the Western slopes of the Pennines in the East and the Yorkshire Dales in the South. It is a region of spectacular scenic diversity held together by its magnificent river system which delineates a geographical framework and embraces a collective Eden entity.

There is also a distinctive sense of identity that has been brought to the area by the people who have lived and worked here for thousands of years. The patchwork of fields, meadows and small woodlands in the valley, contained on all sides by high bare fells and moorland, has been carved out of the original wilderness by generations of farmers. The ancient stone circles, castles, field systems, vernacular buildings, dry stone walls and hedges are the tangible manifestations of Eden's cultural dimension which determine its heritage character.

The Eden landscape is the product of its people and their historic interactions with nature, and this little book features some of the best writers whose work has been inspired by that landscape. Their work is about understanding and communicating feelings. What they see with their eyes they transmit through their hearts.

Dick Capel,
East Cumbria Countryside Project

* Production of this book has been funded by the Heritage Lottery as part of 'Discover Eden', a countryside recreation and interpretation programme managed by East Cumbria Countryside Project in partnership with the Eden Rivers Trust.

Our heartfelt thanks go to all the writers and their representatives, most of whom have generously allowed us to include their poems and prose free of charge, and to Pip Hall for her beautiful linoprints.

The River Eden, Cumberland

EDEN! till now thy beauty had I viewed
By glimpses only, and confess with shame
That verse of mine, whate'er its varying mood,
Repeats but once the sound of thy sweet name:
Yet fetched from Paradise that honour came,
Rightfully borne; for Nature gives thee flowers
That have no rivals among British bowers;
And thy bold rocks are worthy of their fame.
Measuring thy course, fair Stream! at length I pay
To my life's neighbour dues of neighbourhood;
But I have traced thee on thy winding way
With pleasure sometimes by this thought restrained –
For things far off we toil, while many a good
Not sought, because too near, is never gained.

William Wordsworth

The Shaping of Eden

December. Take on the pitch
of the North Star. Look down.
Wait, in a thousand minds. Nothing
is as it seems.

The westward sky's a garden.
Dusk has a pansy bloom,
blueblack, where Venus sets, a soft
diamond sphere;

eastwards on a darkened crest
of hilly cloud, tilting,
armed, moving to the nightly hunt,
Orion stalks.

Far down, an ancient planet
huddles itself to doze
with breathing mountains shrugged and creased
on its chill sides.

What's now, or then? In motion
or at rest? Those valleys –
moments ago ice scoured them through
in buckled plates.

Now, from crannies of the fell
how many becks are sprung
and shining, branched like a handful
of birchtree twigs,

plaiting together, filling,
shaken with pewter light,
alive: nothing seems as it is –
the water corded,

Lowther and Eamont spilling
from tarns and lakes, Belah,
Lyvennet, Leith, Caldew and Roe,
Petteril, Gelt,

Irthing and Croglin Water
streaming, flexed in the shape
of a coral, a spreading tree,
a lightning bolt,

quick veins of the world that pulsed
an age before we lived,
which now we've named and mapped.
Tonight, under the moon,

full Eden slides and curdles
past the nightfolded farms
and the yellow smudge of a town.
Sometimes a star

will wink in the dark of it,
sometimes a salmon splash.
It broadens, meeting the brack, bound
for sands where geese

are speaking in a half-sleep.
Now it unlearns itself
among the firths and islets, all
it has borne down -

rubble, unseated trees, snows,
legends, histories –
lost there in the indifferent sea
that steals all names.

Meg Peacocke

A Descent into Hell Gill

Back in Bernie's café at Ingleton, they had told me to expect an experience somewhere between potholing, swimming, surfing and rock climbing if ever I ventured down the inside of Hell Gill. To find it, I was going to have to trek over the wild moorland of Abbotside Common beyond Wensleydale and Garsdale Head. After an indolent morning in the wilds of Barbondale, I drove up through Garsdale, took the road towards Kirkby Stephen, and parked the car half in Yorkshire, half in Cumbria, astride the county boundary. To walk up the Hell Gill beck on a sunny afternoon out of the vale of the River Eden (of which it is the headwater) was my idea of heaven. There were foxgloves and trout, and a buzzard sailing lazily aloft. From here, the Eden runs north through Appleby to Carlisle, and something odd must have happened in the upheaval of the Ice Age, because Hell Gill is only yards away from the source of the River Ure, which flows the opposite way, to the Humber.

I had packed a rope and wetsuit boots in the rucksack and followed a track over the Settle to Carlisle railway line and uphill past Hell Gill Farm, following the beck to a bridge and a small wood that grows around the precipitous gorge that brought me here. I skirted past it uphill, and there, suddenly, was the entrance to the canyon. The beck just funneled between four rocks and disappeared into the hillside in a steep, concealed cleft. Even from a few yards away, you wouldn't know it was there, and the hidden character of the beck is one possible origin of its name, from the old Teutonic *Hala*, 'the coverer up, or hider', and the verb *hel*, to hide. Looking down into the chasm, listening to the wild clamour of the hissing water pressing forward over the brink, I felt like a child at the top of the helter-skelter, or some equally dubious fairground ride: not at all sure this was such a good idea.

The Hell Gill gorge is like a pothole whose roof has cracked open sixty feet or more above. It plunges almost vertically down the hillside for four hundred yards in a continuous series of waterfalls dropping into overflowing pools of hollowed limestone. Geologically, the tunneling of the limestone probably began at the end of the last Ice Age, 11,000 years ago, when the melt-water from above, finding no other way out, flowed down through alternate strata of limestone, shale and sandstone higher up the hill, and, still trapped by the glacier overhead, burst down a weakness in the limestone layer it encountered here, and bored out the gorge by dissolving the rock.

My temporary state of funk took the form of an impromptu exploration of the upstream beck in the afternoon sun. It forms the county boundary here, and with all the energy of the serious procrastinator, I waded and swam my way upstream, criss-crossing from Yorkshire to Cumbria between huge slabs of grey limestone crammed with fossils. Trout lay in the riffles and darted into shadows. I wallowed in a five-foot-deep waterfall pool, and found vast water-slides, twenty and thirty-foot tablets of the smoothed limestone that was once coral reefs rising out of a tropical seabed 280 million years ago. Here you could bathe all day without meeting a soul, and better still, know in your heart that you would be undisturbed. A hawk had been killing pigeons, butchering them on the rock beside the water here and there. The black stains on the limestone, and stuck feathers, accentuated the desolation of the moor.

Courage up, I returned to the turbulent rim of the gorge and did what I knew might be an unwise thing. I couldn't help it. I began to slide into the mouth of the abyss itself. I found myself in the first of a series of smooth limestone cups four or five feet in diameter and anything between three and five feet deep, stepped at an acute angle down a flooded gulley of hollowed limestone that spiraled into the unknown. In the low light, the smooth, wet walls were a beautiful aquamarine, their shining surface intricately pock-marked like the surface of the moon. All my instincts were to hold on, but to what? The ice and the water had polished everything perfectly. The torrent continually sought to sweep me with it, and so I slithered and climbed down Hell Gill's dim, glistening insides, through a succession of cold baths, in one long primal scream.

There is something atavistic about all swimming, but this was so intensely primitive it was visceral. I felt like Jonah inside the whale. Each time I dropped, or was swept, into a new cauldron, I thought it would be bottomless; the turbulence made the water opaque. Borne down this magical uterus, deafened by the rushing and boiling of the flood, with the sheer rock and just a crack of sky high above me, I felt at once apprehensive and exhilarated. Water was cupped, jugged, saucered, spooned, decanted, stirred and boiled. It was thrown up in a fine spray so you breathed it in, it splashed in your face, it got in your ears, it stung you with its force, it bounced back off every curving surface, it worked unremittingly to sculpt the yielding limestone into the forms of its own well-ordered movement. Beneath the apparent chaos, all this sound and fury conformed to the strict laws of fluid dynamics.

So steep and labyrinthine was the descent that it was impossible to know or see what was to come next. The slippery blue-green wetness and smoothness of everything, and my near-nakedness, only made me more helpless, more like a baby. It was like a dream of being born. Unnamed thunderings like deep, booming heartbeats rose from somewhere below. It was exactly as Frederick Leboyer said in *Birth Without Violence:* 'The horror of being born is the intensity, the immensity of the experience, its variety, its suffocating richness...It is a sensory experience so huge, it is beyond our comprehension.'

Everyone I had talked to about this descent had said that once you're in, you must keep on going down, because you can't climb up. I was glad of the rubber boots and the grip of their soles, but the rope was no use at all because every surface was so perfectly smoothed there was nothing to loop it round. I was conscious that I shouldn't really be doing this alone. I had impetuously broken the first rule of potholing or climbing: that you let somebody know where you're heading before you set out. The feeling became more acute as I reached a waterfall that sounded as if it dropped to Australia, and might be the source of the thundering Pink Floyd 'Atom Heart Mother' effects. They were becoming louder and more insistent.

Suddenly I found myself beneath an overhang of rock. A rope was bolted in here and there, and stretched off into a gloomy void beyond. It was impossible to see where it led, how deep the pool below might be, or how far down. I had no idea where the next foothold was. The torrent just shot over a rocky lip and disappeared from view, into a gothic emptiness. One option was to plunge blindly towards the waterfall and hope to drop into the pool, which might be deep enough for a safe landing. But the voices of reason shouted above the din that I stood an equal chance of being dashed into a rock face. The dilemma, and the stark solitude of my predicament, set my mind racing feverishly.

I considered that for all I knew I might find myself, like the climber in H.G. Well's story 'The Country of the Blind', marooned in a subterranean land full of people like myself who had strayed optimistically down the Hell Gill chasm and stranded themselves beyond the waterfall. I also recalled that in the story, the sightless majority propose to put out the eyes of the newcomer.

I pondered my position carefully, still thinking fast because every minute I spent immobile I was getting wetter and colder. Normally, you would clip on to an overhead rope, but I had no harness. I had met a pair of potholers down by the road and spoken to them briefly. They were accoutred in harnesses, buckles and steel clips like door-to-door ironmongers, and I now cursed my failure to ask them about Hell Gill. Once over the edge and dangling from the rope there was no going back. I would have to go hand over hand down it with fingers that were now half-numb. But how far? I didn't fancy being stuck in a freezing beck all night in swimming trunks. On the other hand I had been told it was impossible to climb back up. Was it really? I wondered. I spent what seemed an eternity fighting my reluctance to turn back and accepting a growing conviction of the logic of at least attempting the ascent. The slight fading of the afternoon light filtering down led me to my decision. I would try going up through the cascading water, and, if I failed, then I would just have to risk going down instead. With the help of strung nerves, the rubber boots, and liberal helpings of adrenalin, I managed to heave myself up the narrow chimney from pool to pool, waterfall to waterfall, against the water. It was slow going, making my way up like a salmon, and I resoved to return some day with a companion, a little more local knowledge, and the right kit.

Emerging at last at the mouth of the gorge, I glanced back at it with faint disbelief and greeted the sky. Then, having dressed, I wandered a little way up the beck in the warm evening and fell asleep on the grass like a new-born babe. I was woken with a jolt by the searing rush of a buzzard stooping on an unwary pigeon. There was a silent explosion of pale grey feathers, like a distant shell. I felt a breath of wind in the grass that could have been a white rabbit hurrying by. 'I've had such a curious dream!' I said to myself, and went off for my tea.

Roger Deakin

Tomorrow's Arrangements

Old Hewitson sat about a lot now and was far past even thistling - for it was the year 1999 - but his memory was perfect. "The last time we had a summer like this," he said, "was 1927, when there was an eclipse of the sun. As there's to be this year. Though whether I'll be turning out to see this one is something still to be thought about."

"You'll see it, Grandpa. We'll carry you on up."

"Carry me on up? Sounds as if you're angels."

"On up on to the top. You know what we mean. We'll all be going. On up above Light Trees for the eclipse."

"You'll not get me up there this time. I'm beyond going up to the Nine Standards."

"Everyone'll be up the Nine Standards. Except the odd crank like old Kendal who's booked his place years ago for Cornwall, where it's to be total."

"Total eclipse," said Grandpa," total eclipse of the sun. They held a total eclipse up here in 1927 on this very spot. Better than it'll be this time where we're a fraction off the track say. In '27 we all got let out of school for it. We had to lie on our backs in t'school yard with little bits of black glass in front of our eyes. We laid out in rows, all laughing on and chit-chattering. There was old Granny Crack's lass lying out next to me in her black woollen stockings and button shoes. Alice Crack she was then from over Kisdon. Bright red hair. By - she was a talker. She changed. 'Alice Crack,' she said - the school teacher - 'Alice Crack, if you don't stop talking, we'll all go inside and you won't any of you see it and if you don't see it now you'll never see it for there won't be another until 1999 and that one won't be total.' 'Don't see why I shouldn't see that 'un,' says Alice Crack, 'I'll be scarcely ninety. You won't see it though, will you, Miss?' So she had to go inside and she didn't see it. She had to sit at her desk. She cried an'all."

"Well, she'll see it this time," said Mrs Teesdale. "We promised we'd take her. Lord knows how. Maybe in a pram. She's a fair weight yet, too."

"I don't ever see," said Poppet who was over for hay-time from down the road, her husband being up the fell all day with the rest – "why it's got to be up at the Nine Standards we have to do things."

"Always was," said her mother-in-law, "it's a tradition."

"Time some traditions was looked over and sorted out," said old Hewitson. "Traipsing here and there. The Jubilee - all the Jubilees. King Charles's wedding. The old Queen Mother's funeral. Why some of them still goes up for Guy Fawkes to this day."

"Old Mr Kendal says that people have gone up there since before the Romans," said Poppet. "He says the Nine Standards are probably Roman soldiers turned to stone. Says its part of the Lost Legion of the Ninth they used to write about in the old children's books. They never got to Scotland, Mr Kendal said. They only got as far as the Rigg and got turned to stone."

"Kendal," said Old Hewitson, "always read over-many fond books."

"He says before the Romans the Rigg is where the Celts used to drive their cattle through the smoke."

"That," said Grandpa Hewitson, "is pure ridiculous Kendal talk. No folks, not even Romans, was daft enough to take cattle up yonder."

"For sacrifice and that," said Poppet's girl, Anne.

"It'd be sacrifice all right, sacrificing good money int' market. They'd be good for nowt, hiked all the way up to them Nine Standards and put through smoke."

"Nor us neither going gowking at eclipses of the sun eleven o'clock in the morning of a good day's hay-making," said Bell, coming in to see after the baskets setting off. "I'm warning you I'm not going looking at eclipses on August whatever 'tis. I'm cracking on."

"You'll not get much done int' dark."

"It's not going to last five minutes."

"There's the coming and going of it. And its bad luck not to take notice."

"It'll be darkness all right," said Old Hewitson.

"All darkness is darkness."

"No. Darkness is all sorts. And let me tell you, Bell, darkness from eclipses of the sun is not like owt else. It's neither darkness of night nor gloom of twilight nor darkness from the Helm Wind over Dufton, like there can be on a bright day."

"Darkness is darkness. I don't care about missing out on seeing some darkness."

"There's more'n darkness about it. Stars come out. You can spot the planets - Venus, Mercury. Birds stop singing. All animals up at Light Trees from Hartley Birket to Nateby Birket will be falling silent and standing mazed."

"Aye well. I dare say we'll not ignore it, Grandpa."

"And another thing I remember. Lying there int' school yard. Under them currant bushes she kept. You remember them currant bushes, Bell?"

"Not there in my time, Grandpa. Nor yet in Dad's."

"Well under these currant bushes and the two-three trees they had there was little wee bits o' light scattered. For an hour before, maybe. Little pieces like of light, and as the sky changed to like sunset, every little speckle under them trees turned crescent-shaped like the

17

new moon."

"There'll not be yon up the Nine Standards. There's not a tree to speak of. And Standards themselves is too solid to show any crescent moons scattered about."

"Which is why I'll be staying down here," said Old Hewitson. "I'll seat myself int' garden by Mary's lupins. Alice Crack, the Egg Witch, can go gallivanting in prams."

"Anyways, it'll likely rain," said Bell, who had grown over the years more like his father than his father had ever been. "Like it's about to do today. Come on. Let's get moving. It's nine o'clock already."

"In my day," said Old Hewitson, "hardest part of hay-time was over by nine o'clock of a morning. That's when we rested, nine o'clock, horses being tired out. Good fast go at it we had from five int' morning till eight. Then breakfast. In the hedge back. Tatie pies. You could only cut properly with dew upon the ground. People got out of their beds them days. I were called out at five from under my bedroom window. I were earning by time I were eleven."

"You's talking of scything days."

"I'se talking of horses. Same as it's horses again now. There was scything and leading with horses, then cutting and leading with horses. Then away went the horses and in came the machinery. And now, since the oil went, we're back to the horses. I never thought I'd live to see the old tractors go. Grand they were, though dangerous. Rolled on you many times more often than any horse if you didn't handle them right. I liked the old tractors mind. Historic."

Jane Gardam

Ravenstonedale Park

Circling, crying to their startled chicks to lie
doggo, the curlew pair would discourage me
from resting here; but this steep gill had beckoned
 even up wall-lined lanes,

when by St.Helen's Well I set a swift pace,
bowled up Hawking Scar, followed burrowed grassy
dyke-mounds on to Scandal Beck, till straight before
 me Gallows Hill,

and blocking the Dale the buttress of Wild Boar.
How each name gives an ancient secret away!
Here St. Gilbert's English cannons cured and fished,
 guardians of the well

and parish sanctuary bell, skilled archery
at Chapel Butts, left strip lynchets on the Riggs.
Ahead, the high stone wall the thwarted tenants
 built for Wharton

and his drove of deer: farewell slabs they slotted
as they took inferior plots outside the Park
by Thornthwaite, Stonely and the Mires. Yet flowers,
 fellsides are the same

as when that throng whose forms line in our graveyards
strode these slopes, for both cotton-sedge and tormentil
seen at my feet today have seeded, rooted
 down those hay-turned years,

while Metcalfes, Fothergills and Dents home here still.
How different for those former folk not borne
by Newbiggin Coffin lane, crouched skeletons
 unearthed near the Severals,

diggers of the Dyke, whose craggy settlement
far up behind me looked back to Ewe Fell Coum,
eyed beyond a denser, wooded horizon:
    Wild Boar birches,

Green Bell oaks and hazels; for a turbary
once delved out proffered shell, catkin and kernel,
with caried roots, acorns deep in the moss-growth.
    Along such scrub Sir Thomas

Musgrave harried the last tusked boar near the Nab.
But who scorns Time, or cannot tell the tenor
of those voices, measures from the ancient air,
    the creak of wheel or mill,

the Market Day chatter in the old Black Swan?
Those only who forget that Time anneals us,
quested silence speaks, that from our family's past
    we fault the present,

how to know the tracks, the names and the tackle
is to belong, to share in a memory
that searches further than the scan of one mind,
    one assertion.

Though imagination fuses much detail,
those tales the Old can tell thrive in the hearer,
make us feel our fathers kept the key to joy,
    a loss of innocence,

yet give us fine companions. May our customs
too have descendants marvel at the teller
and share the romp and rhythm of our praises,
    our choicest moments!

As now I whoop in the dance to Jimmy Fawcett's
fiddle, scour Coldbeck for Maggie and her ducks,
fetch meat from Blacket, lead horses carting corn
    from Dixon's yard

plying the storms they stood, the hauls for shelter,
I feel the present shine with those precious lives
and skills, as now this July sky does after
    dull morning's rain.

The late sun beams light-shafts down on Harter Fell
and rising I glory in a dearer sense
of home, head on northward past the Giants' Graves
    to Smardale Bridge

musing at what occasion gave us Nettle Gill
or Breakyneck Scar; till turning to the fells
at fresher cries, I see the parent curlews
    wheel and glide to land.

Michael Ffinch

The running changes

Driving northward in February once
on the run, to be clear of the Midlands
in a panic and ruin of life

I heard the telephones ring in the air
for the first hundred miles.

But in the afternoon rain I found Sedbergh
and threaded on through it,
a silent close stone lock
which let me pass but barred my trouble;
I feared only it might be gone on ahead
to lie in wait for me by the Tyne. Then
the look of the road up to Kirkby,
the plainness and dark of it, settled
my stomach; and the sight of Brough
Keep, black as could be, risen in the fields
by a change of road, made me for that day
my own man, out over cold stripped Stainmore.

Another year,
coming down in peace out of Durham
in a late snowstorm towards sunset

I met the lorries, headlamps full on,
thrashing their way up over Stainmore
in spray-wave of rose-tinged slush,
cloud-world behind and below them
filling the valley-bottom,
rolling, shot through with pink,
in the side-valleys breaking apart
to lance the pastures right across
with sunlight from no sure source:

and under the last trail of the cloud,
the vanishing up of its blush
into the grey, and the snow thinning,
there, once again, was Brough Castle
marking the turn southward
and being dark.

Roy Fisher

Shap

The name confronts you –
a wind with a wet slap in it
leathering the fell,

flapping black oilskins,
spitting at squinting eyes.
Ewes bunch at the wall,

the collie slinks low,
scuds between gusts,
blown by the skirling whistle.

Two crows are blots
on fence posts. On barbed wire,
clots and wisps of course wool.

White plumes torn from the quarry.
Fieldfares shucked from a thorn tree,
nowhere to settle.

The buzzer blares. The dull boom.
A wind with a clap of thunder in it,
stamping its boot on Shap Fell.

Mick North

Isaac

In March the running water of the valley is bitter, acid cold, as snow on the fells begins to melt and is brought down over chilled rocks and icy beds. It has in it all the breaking soul of winter, thousands of dying flakes in one long, moving water coffin. But despite the cold, the streams and waterfalls are very clear, clearer than they have been all year, a perfect window into the living houses of the river. Sediment and detritus are bound to the ground, cauterized by ice, and are unable to dissolve into the passing liquid until the thaw takes a better hold in April, loosening the old skin of the earth, allowing it to shed.

Isaac lies half on the ground, half braced on a rock over a channel of the river. His face in the water turns purple and yellow and his lips soon numb. If he is not careful, his muscles will start to spasm uncontrollably and he will lose his balance, shocking the rest of his body into the water, electric cold. He times himself within the icy cataracts. He has perhaps no more than ten seconds before his cheeks begin to roll of their own accord, as if he is fitting, then he must surface. Knowing the direction of flow, he turns his face downstream, using his head to block its package, protecting his eyes from the burn of the moving current. He opens their lids. There is a second when their mechanism falters, they will not adjust to the temperature, having lost the slim warmth of an eyelid covering, the lenses will not still and focus is impossible. Then, the panic subsides. Pupils retract. The world of the inside river appears, detailed and precise.

Water is white-clear. And after a while it is non-existent. There is no wetness. There is no thin element rushing past, only frigid movement, arctic winds in another planet's sky.

He sees sharply, down to the rocks on the riverbed, and a prehistoric tail, a grey crayfish leg is tucking itself under a dolmen. He reaches down with a quiet hand and turns the rock over without so much as a particle of soil or sand lifting into the current of the river. The crayfish, a dark lobster-cat, does not move. Its whisker antennae, sensitive enough to feel a shift of life a foot away in the water, twitch, touch-sighted, its pincers gather energy. It knows the house is gone. Isaac moves a small hand through the current quick as a diving birds and pinches it on the armoured back at the point where it cannot reach a claw back to him. It kicks its tail, flicking back into the firm grip. The divisions of its shell click against each other, the sound dull underwater. He loves that sensation, the language of sound. He turns it over, examines the pale-grey underbelly, the alien anatomy riddled with legs, then drops it into the wind to watch it swim backwards under the shifted rock, to continue sleeping in the river. He puts his fingers in his mouth, sucks them, moving his tongue, as if to create a friction of heat. But his is not a fish-blood, there is no oil under his skin to keep him warm in the river's cataracts.

Ten seconds have passed. His teeth are moving against his cheek. Cold invades every pore of skin with tiny arrows. He ignores the sensation of spears a few seconds longer.

Trout gape at him. Their spots shimmering fire, locked with brown-silver and lit by the water's light. Minnows butting the current, all eyes. The black silk of a hidden eel. Crustaceans adding sections to their shells along the cratered stones of the river valley walls. It is all worthwhile.

The houses are filled with life even in winter, reptilian, marine, and the fish, sluggish in the near-zero climate. All is stark at this time of year, barren, before the sun warms reeds and algae to life from the rich beds, and grassland returns once more in the river, forestation, jungle, beating slowly in the benthic weathers. But now, life gives itself up utterly for observation.

He will stay down for as long as he can, a watery pioneer, caught between two worlds. His foreign body, learning the river's tricks. His nostrils closing, eyes in stasis, not giving away a suggestion of life, no tell-tale air bubble struggling to the surface to reveal his presence. His blood crystallizes, congeals. His lips turn blue and their cells die. But he will cut into the water again and again for the pleasure of the other world, a boy tranquillizing his face. His head smashing through the reflection of a lumbering crow in the sky. Because the March water is sparkling and icy and pure, a conductor of vision, a magnifying glass to all corners of the pools. A rare month for spying on these inhabitants, the strange and beautiful nations.

He holds his body out of the stream, better to preserve a supply of warmth, though the ground and rock under him steals at it. He allows a hand now and again into the water like a wingless bird diving for silver, keeping the other on a slippery, moss-covered stone above the river, which still has little pieces of ice tucked tight in its fur.

The crayfish is a good find, time-consuming, but he remains submerged for over fifteen seconds, unwilling to neglect other species in their tender cages.

Then the pain begins to dissolve all other sensation in his head and his eye rolls back to life. Spasms rock his flesh and he surfaces. Coming up, the air seems even colder than the water. The mountain breeze licks at his dripping ears, nips at them with quick bites, his forehead smarts. He breathes, unable to prevent a dry, clamped cough from coming up as the oxygen is taken into the halted lungs. He massages his neck and throat. The glands have tight knots. His wet collar has begun to freeze, stiffening against his neck, and chafing. He unbuttons the shirt, folds it off his skin. He puts the cold-staved fingers of his right hand under his tongue again but there is no heat left for either to borrow.

~

At least once or twice a day Isaac will come here to do this. In the summer he will swim down to the riverbed, wholly submerged, and in the winter he'll break ice to feel water on his forehead. Even though his mother will scold him for the damp clothing and his frozen hands. He'll tell her that God has made a botched job, that he should have been a fish, and his mother will scold him for that, too. But she knows it, really, that he cannot keep away from water. That he is mesmerized by it. Ella has set firm in her mind the notion that her son will meet his fate in the waters of the Mardale valley, though he swims well enough. That one day she will find his corpse, a pale bag locked full of water at the bottom of Hop Grumble ghyll, where the torrent meets the lake. Or that Samuel will have to wade out under the Measand bridge, grope a hand between the reeds and find a son. She has her visions, her omens. The drowned wasp suspended in a jar of honey, a silver birch leaf fallen into a puddle. She tries to explain the dangers to him, to encourage him into other habits. He will not be swayed. He is called to the river. Because there he has the freedom to fly, weightless and sighted through the currents of the valley's water. It is a better world, where life is slower and quicker at once, and there is silence except for the movement of the river's atmosphere itself.

~

After a while Isaac stands, turns down the path, dizzy and rigid with cold. Today he has stayed down too long. There are side-effects to his devotion of the river. Bright stars of yellow light are imploding near the corners of his eyes. His peripheral vision is destroyed. The horizon is dull and its lines are separating, closing together, separating. He stumbles, sits down on a rock, rubs the last of the river out of his eyes, crushing his palms' heels into the sockets, smashing out frost and winter tears.

An impossible creature is just ahead of him, steaming on the roadside. A red dragon, maybe fourteen feet long. And beside it a man made of dark-green panels. The lines around the beast and the man chase and flex. It is a picture in a dream, an illustration from a medieval book made modern, a hallucination. As if the peculiar effects of the river have begun freezing the soft tissues inside his head. He does not trust his eyes, which are banging with light. But no, hallucinations are reserved for fevers, diseases. The river does not make him sick. He rubs his sockets, crushing yellow stars against his skull, opens his eyes, blinks. And blinks again. No, a dragon, definitely. Dragon.

~

When the man in the suit saw Isaac he thought at first that the boy was sick. He was pale and dripping with sweat. His shirt was dark with it. He did not seem stable and was swaying on the rock where he sat, staring intently straight ahead, but without seeing what his eyes offered up, it seemed. His hair had separated into bright blond icicles.

The man took a few steps towards the boy, as if to catch him if he fell. But he jumped up from the rock.

- Don't run.

The boy stood for a moment, swaying, then sat again with a sudden jerky movement. The gesture seemed unrelated to the request.

The man walked slowly up the steep path towards him, holding one hand in front of him as if to urge calmness, to dissuade flight. As if approaching a stray of some kind.

- There's no need for running. No need at all. Just stay, and I'll come to you.

Isaac squinted up one eye, bearing his teeth on that side of his face as his mouth followed upwards after the squint. There was a terrible pain behind that eye, a narrow, tunnel hole of pain going back towards his skull. An ache of bone. Ice-pain. The man sat next to him, flipping up the back of his suit jacket as he sat.

- You're soaked. Are you unwell?

- No, I'm well enuff.

There was a brief silence, during which Isaac sniffled loudly. The man wondered whether he should offer the boy a handkerchief to dry himself with, blow his nose, but decided against it. They sat for a time quietly, without talking, a damp, cold boy in a wet shirt and a man who looked as if he would be more at home in the offices of Piccadilly or Manhattan, not the lake country. Both were dressed in wholly unsuitable attire, respectively out of place in the wintry environment.

- What d'yer want?

- Well, nothing, really. I just thought you might be unwell. You looked poorly.

- I'm grand as owt.

- You're shivering.

- Aye, so'd you be, if you'd bin in t'beck.

- Did you fall in?

The boy grunted as if annoyed, as if the man had suddenly become very stupid and had asked a ridiculous question. He coughed without putting a hand over his mouth. His body was shaking.

- You mean you went in voluntarily? That's a bit irregular at this time of year, isn't it? Won't your mother be angry? Won't she scold you?

- Shi'll not if she dun't know.

- Oh. Of course. Well, rest assured you can count on my complete discretion.

The man in the suit put out his hand, paused, then laid it on the boy's wrist.

- You're frozen. You feel like ice cream, you look about as pale as ice cream, too.

Then the man laughed. His laugh was full of genuine mirth and there were small, fine lines around his eyes.

- Well, what's your name?

- T's Isaac.

- Pleased to make your acquaintance, Isaac. I'm Jack.

The boy hopped off the rock and turned to face the man. He stuck out a hand in a blunt gesture. He was still squinting one eye savagely. They shook, the older of the two charmed by the unexpected manners of the boy.

- Well Isaac, I'm a little concerned with how cold that hand is.

- Warmin' up.

- Yes. But, if it's right with you, I'll put my coat on you and escort you home in case you melt. Where do you live? One of the farms?

The boy shook his head quickly, sending a spray of icy water out from his hair like a dog shaking after retrieving a thrown stick from a lake. He pushed away the offered coat.

- Cum wid us, if y'like, but I'll not wear it. Shi'll know.

- Yes, your mother might be a problem. Tell you what, then, put it on now and take it off when we get close to the house, before she spies you. She'll be none the wiser. Do we have a deal?

Isaac considered the proposal for a moment. It seemed fair enough. The man noticed how pale his non-squinting eye was, almost clear apart from a faint bluish smudge around the pupil. He found the child a little disarming to look at. The boy took the coat and put it on, struggling with its size. The arms almost reached the ground and its shoulders drooped off his back. The man buttoned up the front, though it made little difference for a snug fit. Under his jacket the man had on a pale-yellow shirt with gold armbands on his biceps. Isaac reached out and touched the one on his left arm.

- Whatter them for?

-To stop my arms from falling off. How's the coat? Better?

- Feels like rabbuts' ears, eh?

- Rabbits' ears?

Isaac went over to the water, dropped to his knees and hunted around for a second in the grass. The man winced as the coat was knelt into the earth. Then Isaac came back over, holding out a small green and white leaf. The man took it. It was long and slightly concave, covered with downy hairs, similar in shape and texture to a rabbit's ear. The reference made sense. The boy was grinning and seemed pleased at the lesson he was giving about flora. He snatched the plant back and began to tickle a palm with it as he walked away. He walked clumsily and with tripping steps down the steep path towards the red car. The man followed.

- Yor t'fella that's gunna mek lake bigga.
- Yes, I am.

Sarah Hall

Reflections

Near the source of the River Eden, an eccentric Victorian erected a stone with a carved Greek inscription that begins: 'Seek the river of the soul - whence it springs . . .' I often think of it as I look out of my window at the Eden flowing past - little more than twenty miles from William Mounsey's stone, but already a powerful force. The soul is now a rather unfashionable concept, but it's still a convenient label for that part of ourselves that defies biological definition, and is the source of our creativity. That the river and the soul should be twinned comes as no surprise - from the beginning of human existence rivers have been regarded as mystical and numinous. For primitive people the sight of water trickling out of a rock was a miraculous, life-giving event. So fundamental is the association that the words for river and birth - and sometimes for the birth canal itself - are the same in many old languages. It has also been used as a symbolical or mythological conduit into the underworld - the realms of death. The river is a good, if overused, metaphor, not only for all things spiritual, but also for the narrative journey of life itself.

The word Eden has associations of paradise, though the name was given to this river in another language where the syllables meant something else. Eden is on my birth certificate and Eden is where I now live, in an old mill perched on the bank of the river where it enters a natural gorge between sandstone cliffs at the Bongate end of Appleby. I can watch the river's variations through my window as I write, the delicate patternings of light and shade, the constant changes of mood. The murmur of the weir provides a continuing soundscape through every night and day. I know the riverbank intimately. When I wake in the morning I can watch herons disputing territory above the weir, red squirrels bolting across the footbridge, spawning salmon in the gravel beds. Once on a deserted morning a family of three otters walked along the foot of the weir - and once we surprised a bird of prey lifting a duckling off the water. It's a source of continuing fascination and delight.

The riverside at Bongate is a beautiful, peaceful place, but it hasn't always been so. The mill stands on an ancient way, guardian of an important ford over the River Eden. The hollow lane that leads down to the ford has been trodden some seven feet deep below the level of the land by a vast procession of long-forgotten people who've walked this way for thousands of years since the end of the last Ice Age.

Living here I feel very close to the flow of human history. Mills have stood here for a long time and the foundations of the weir date back to Roman times. Modern repairs gouge up blackened oak beams as well as more recent medieval masonry. Local archaeologists have told me that there would once have been an altar to the gods of river and track-way, where travellers could make offerings before they crossed the ford. There would have been no shortage of travellers either - all east to west traffic across Stainmore came through Appleby. It was probably the equivalent of the 'last homely house' before the wild uplands of the Pennines.

After the Romans, the Vikings came up river, fighting, farming and fishing. They built a little church here on the 'holme field' opposite the mill, according to one source. The Vikings often built their churches over the sites of pagan worship and the ford over the river at Bongate seems to have been just such a place. After two restorations, little remains of the original church now - parts of a hog-back tomb taken away to a museum, some exquisitely carved masonry incorporated into the wall above one of the nave windows. But the Vikings gave their name to Appleby and one of the most valuable Viking finds in Britain, the Ormside Chalice, was excavated a couple of miles up-river from the mill.

Born in the peaceful second half of the 20th century I find it difficult to imagine living on marginal land fought and bargained over and repeatedly laid waste. But over the next two hundred years Appleby was overrun by Norman invaders only to be burned and pillaged by the Scots, then re-taken by the English, before plague decimated the entire area - thinning out what the marauders had left. By the 14th century all was 'ruin and desolation' in and around Appleby. Even more recently, in 1745, Clifton Moor was the location of the last battle on English soil between Bonnie Prince Charlie's Scottish army and that of the Duke of Cumberland. The Highlanders were defeated and then massacred and eyewitnesses spoke of bodies floating in the river and the tragic rounding up of those who had escaped into the surrounding countryside. Many of those captured were not professional soldiers but either young boys or old men, as recorded by a local observer.

'I saw the poor wretches brought into Appleby, little, ill-looking creatures, their heads and feet quite bare, and the most wretched rags on the rest of their bodies, far from sufficient to cover them . . . scoffed and hooted at by the rabble which ran in multitudes about them, their feet all wreathed with clods of mire, mixed with blood; ready to faint with hunger and the horror of their condition . . . ' It's hard to think of the kind of atrocities we see beamed from distant countries to our television screens taking place here.

But the river too, like its history, has a dark side. In winter it metamorphoses into a brown monster - scouring the river banks on either side, submerging the garden and the car park, rising up the front steps, before bullying its way through the doorway into the cellars. Three or four times in ten years it's risen high enough to flow through the whole ground floor. This has been a terrifying experience; the mill is suddenly in the middle of the river, buffeted by tons of water surging through windows and doors. The sheer force of it is awesome. But the mill was built to take the river - a sturdy industrial structure disguised by an elegant Georgian facade that looks more Italian than Cumbrian, built by a continental architect after the great flood of 1822 - which must say something cautionary about its predecessor!

I look up from my office window to Appleby Castle high on the cliff above the river - and this is how it was intended, since the mill was owned by the castle and Bongate takes its name from the bondmen who lived there in their insanitary hovels, fording the river to gain access to the castle. I like to think, as I tap out words on my computer keyboard, of that other, earlier authoress who lived there and put pen to paper in the 17th century. Diaries and letters were the only valid forms of writing for women four hundred years ago - anything else was presumption or immorality. 'Men are for the public, women for the private sphere,' one man wrote, reprovingly and with devastating accuracy. The few women who dared to publish their writings in small private editions circulated among friends were often castigated as whores. The surviving diary of that great non-conformist Lady Anne Clifford is a source of great delight. Reading it I can't help wondering what she might have done without the constraints of the time.

This has been a place of strong women. In the 14th as in the 17th century it was a woman who ordered things. Elizabeth Clifford, whose husband died in the crusades in 1393, was granted the sheriffwick of Westmorland in her own right and lived at Appleby Castle for thirty years. Her medieval tomb in Bongate church was inexplicably broken up when Anne Clifford restored the church and the fragments of her effigy were incorporated into the wall, until 1886 when they were rediscovered and reassembled. I often go to look at her tomb and wish that I knew more about her life story and why her monument was so viciously destroyed. Unfortunately, unlike her descendant Lady Anne, she left no diaries or letters to provide clues to the mystery.

Surrounded by history and beauty, supported by such role models, what better place could there be for a writer to live? But sometimes the scenery is more of a distraction than a source of inspiration and it's more tempting to leave my desk and walk up the river than to pick up a pen. As I walk I often think of the words of Richard Jeffries, 19th century author and visionary, confronted by `that far space, full of soul-secrets . . . ` No one could express so eloquently that state of ecstasy engendered by being alone in a wild and beautiful place. `Everything around is supernatural; everything so full of unexplained meaning. . . . From earth and sea and sun, from night, the stars, from day, the trees, the hills, from my own soul - I stand this moment . . . face to face with nature, face to face with the supernatural, with myself. My naked mind confronts the unknown.'

Kathleen Jones

Daffodils

I WANDERED lonely as a cloud
That floats on high o'er vales and hills,
When all at once I saw a crowd,
A host of golden daffodils:
Along the lake, beneath the trees,
Fluttering and dancing in the breeze.

Continuous as the stars that shine
And twinkle on the milky way,
They stretched in never-ending line
Along the margin of a bay:
Ten thousand saw I at a glance,
Tossing their heads in sprightly dance.

The waves beside them danced, but they
Out-did the sparking waves in glee:
A poet could not but be gay,
In such a jocund company:
I gazed-and gazed–but little thought
What wealth the show to me had brought:

For oft, when on my couch I lie
In vacant or in pensive mood,
They flash upon that inward eye
Which is the bliss of solitude;
And then my heart with pleasure fills,
And dances with the daffodils.

William Wordsworth

The River

In my first sleep
I came to the river
and looked down
through the clear water –
only in dream
water was so pure,
laced and undulant
lines of flow
on its rocky bed
water of life
streaming for ever.

A house was there
beside the river
and I, arrived,
an expected guest
about to explore
old gardens and libraries –
but the car was waiting
to drive me away.

One last look
into that bright stream –
trout there were
and clear on the bottom
monster form
of the great crayfish
that crawls to the moon.
On its rocky bed
living water
in whorls and ripples
flowing unbended.

There was the car
to drive me away.
We crossed the river
of living water –
I might not stay,
but must return
by the road too short
to the waiting day.

In my second dream
pure I was and free
by the rapid stream,
my crystal house the sky,
the pure crystalline sky.

Into the stream I flung
a bottle of clear glass
that twirled and tossed and spun
in the water's race
flashing the morning sun.

Down that swift river
I saw it borne away,
my empty crystal form,
exultant saw it caught
into the current's spin,
the flashing water's run.

                    Kathleen Raine

Cockley Moor, Dockray, Penrith

Outside, the cubist fells are drawn again
beneath the light that speaks ex tempore;
the fur of bracken thickens in the rain
and wrinkles shift upon the scurfy scree.

Inside, like tiles the poet's pleasures lie,
square laid on circle, circle laid on square,
and pencilled angles of eternity
are calculated on the double stair.

Outside, the curlew gargles through the mist,
the mountain pansies shut up shop and fade,
the wheatear chisels with his crystal fist,
and day on day like stone on stone is laid.

Inside, are cows on canvas, painted broom
fresh as a girl's thin fingers burst to flower,
bright leaves that do not fall, but fence the room
with the arrested growth of a June hour.

The curving cloud embellishes the sky,
the geometric rain slants to the corn;
inside, a man remembers he must die,
outside, a stone forgets that it was born.

Norman Nicholson

While the poor gather round

WHILE the Poor gather round, till the end of time
May this bright flower of Charity display
It's bloom, unfolding at the appointed day;
Flower than the loveliest of the vernal prime
Lovelier – transplanted from heaven's purist clime!
"Charity never faileth:" on that creed,
More than on written testament or deed,
The pious Lady built with hope sublime.

William Wordsworth

Spells Of The Raven

Split a speel and I am there.
Lift a stane and I am there.

Who provides for the Hrafn his food?
Seavy Sike and Longtongue Beck.
Hungry heath and busy dod.

Yet shall I run in the russet squirrel,
above the ferns in the oaks and the mizzle.

Neither walking nor flying,
I'm gang hame to the Eden.

Split a speel and I am there.
Lift a stane and I am there.

Who provides for the Hrafn his food?
Skelling Moor and Hrafnwic Fell.
Butter flosh and bedlam crag.

Yet shall I run in the birch white trout,
in the chalk clear burn and the kikkling rout.

Neither clothed nor bare,
I'm gang hame to the Eden.

Split a speel and I am there.
Lift a stane and I am there.

Who provides for the Hrafn his food?
Flowering Wood and Jordan Hills.
Goodie feld and beggaram dun.

Yet shall I run in the kraking Hrafn,
counsel the soul of the resting hound swain.

Neither black nor white,
I'm gang hame to the Eden.

Split a speel and I am there.
Lift a stane and I am there.

Who provides for the Hrafn his food?
Appleby Street and Kirkoswald.
Skinny brant and paradise clough.

Yet shall I run in the red scar berry.
Summer will come and the thorns gang merry.

Neither followed nor alone,
I'm gang hame to the Eden.

Split a speel and I am there.
Lift a stane and I am there.

Josephine Dickinson

Below the Ridge

below the ridge
above wind inscribed stone
drop shadowed in moss

a buzzard splays
                    stilled wind
and lifts,
in the cold updraft
of the valley's steep incline,
a hung moment

dark clouds contour pale
a glow of veiled sun
in hail in hill fog
thickens mist with light

like my heart
a lark starts up
its striding song
long on pauses
flaffs a fast wind forward

sheep trails entwine the west face
a hare breaks
            as though, I thought

Tom Pickard

Faces in the rock

The Devonian rock that curls round the Solway like the head of a shepherd's crook makes a stone - especially the Old Red Sandstone - that looks warm and lit even on days of grim overcast. It was used in the houses of Brampton in Cumbria and Annan in Dumfriesshire. It towers above the secret beaches of the Eden between Lazonby and Armathwaite. In mid-winter unmelting grains of a light snowfall are sprinkled like salt on a brown mulch of oak leaves. At midday a lemony sun wins through and warms us enough to climb with our jerseys off.

A staircase of rocks green as marzipan and roots like bared tendons leads down to the main beach. The Eden swims past, full and silent. At the edge of the main cliff with its grotesque scoops, we swing out over the water and up into the woods via beaks of sandstone and limbs of oaks twisted by their efforts to stay rooted in the barely stable loam. The route's name, Kingfisher, almost persuades me that I've seen the sapphire glints of one skimming upstream. It is certainly dipper and heron country. The best we can be is squirrels, at home among these looping roots and branches, or otters slithering along the river's margin, half in half out of the water.

The river is almost never low enough here to give dry access to a unique fastness. If you pick the right oak from which to abseil, you can work your way down to a little beach of coarse brown grains, smoothed by floods. A face looks out at you from the sandstone, larger than human, terracotta and naked as a flowerpot, with grooves to represent a drooping moustache and pecked dots to represent eyebrows. It is in no convention, not Olympian, not heroic, not grotesque, neither goblin nor god and too baldly mask-like to be quite a man. It is simply what the fairly soft and brittle rock made possible for the more or less skilled chisel of the Eden Valley craftsman. 'Make faces,' said the squire - William Mounsey perhaps, who also liked to commission ornaments for the village houses downstream - and here is what he made.

Other heads stare at you from the rough natural rock nearby. A pair, almost like a two-headed cherub puffing out wind in the corner of a 17th-century map. A single one whose situation below a draining of earthy moisture has let lichens blotch his features, making them dark and ill. I say 'his.' What gender have we here, if any? The moustache is unmistakable. The other faces are sexless. They are not Narcissus, son of a blue Nymph and a River-god, nor are they Naiads, from their palace deep under the river Peneios in the Vale of Tempe. They do not look like relatives of the goddess Coventina, 35 kilometres away along the Roman Wall at Chesters, whose forearm grows into a water-lily stem, or the water-nymphs from the same site whose skirts curve into folds like solution channels grooved down sandstone or limestone. These Armathwaite faces are just their own quaint selves.

The Classical possibilities are not irrelevant. Great trouble has been taken to chisel a text on a plain slab nearby. It ends with the line ἄριστος μεν ὕδωρ, the best water - a copywriter's slogan, as though someone had been trying to sell off the Eden to a Greek entrepreneur. (The way things are going, this may happen yet.). The text on the slab is the kind of late imitation of an ode by Horace that the bygone gentry so often had inscribed when they wanted to make a statement:

Oh the fishers gentle life
Happiest is of any
Void of pleasur full of strife
And belovd by many
Other joys are but toys
And to be lamented
Only this a pleasure is
Timber Fishing
ἄριστος μεν ὕδωρ
Eden IB
1855

The mis-spelling, the lettering which reverses many of the s's and n's, the broken-off stanza - these smack of a pretended sub-literacy or hamfistedness. It's rustick, consciously rough.

Perhaps Mounsey (if it was he) was being equally pawky in situating his river-shrine in a spot where almost nobody would ever see it. To exchange looks with the Faces, you must be determined, you must dangle in and climb back out, or wade along like a salmon fisherman or a poacher. The last time I was there, my dog Hardy was frantic to reach us. He knocked branches and clods down on to our heads, then got down to the water further along and plunged back upstream to the beach, almost out of his depth. As we left him again, to climb back out, he displaced his worry into furious scrabbling with his chiselly paws. Pounds of sand were spraying backwards into the river. After he had gone a robin arrived, mistaking the place for a freshly dug plot, and searched fruitlessly for worms. The beach was as trampled and gouged out as a football pitch. No doubt by now the Eden has flooded and smoothed it out again.

David Craig

Eden Holds Me in Thrall

Eden: voluptuous hills, wooded valleys, wild, bleak uplands, soaring veined red sandstone cliffs, plunging gorges and a river – a mighty river - at its pounding heart. This is a rich and diverse land, bound and seamed by watery threads, an endless tracery of becks and ghylls lacing the land and feeding the insatiable thirst of the mother river. The river is a paradox, a constant yet forever in flux, always moving yet sometimes motionless. The marketing man's simple silhouette of hill and lake has no place here; no trite logo can define this riverside world.

Look across the jigsaw of the Eden gorge, in the early morning when a single strand of gossamer–mist traces the route of the river or at evening when a fatally wounded sun bleeds into a distant horizon and even the worst excesses of modern man, the quasi-urban sprawls, hacienda bungalows extended to within inches of their own boundaries and modern agribusiness' monstrous green tin sheds are – for now – reduced to bit part roles on the vast theatrical stage of Eden's splendour.

Here at Ainstable – its name comes from the Norse for bracken covered slopes - man's resourcefulness and skill has turned barren hillside into viable, productive pasture. There are other historical footprints too: the breathtaking Carlisle to Settle railway and its imposing sandstone viaducts; limestone kilns like small cathedrals high up on Croglin fell; the remains of ancient gypsum mines near Long Meg and her daughters - the mysterious, vaguely unsettling stone circle at Langwathby; Lacey's Caves that may have been a winestore or – and I prefer this interpretation – a grotto of faux romanticism inhabited by a rented hermit. Armathwaite had no need of an impostor-hermit for its own, living in his clearing, gave the settlement its name Ermithwaite. Just up river is Nunnery House, the site of a Benedictine nunnery founded in 1089 and where, in 1775, Christopher Aglionby laid out the enchanting Nunnery Walks although these are now closed to the public. That tourist riff-raff are now excluded from the bewitching Croglin Water, with its tiny perfect gorge and spectacular waterfall – surely one of Eden's most romantic tributaries – at least means that Wordsworth's spirit sleeps more peacefully: "What change shall happen next to Nunnery

Dell? Canal and Viaduct and Railway, tell!" wailed Wordsworth at the prospect of having to share his beloved walks. Years ago, when Nunnery Walks were still open, there was a rope and wood swing right down by the shore where you could sway absorbing the silence of a secret Eden: I wonder if it's still there.

The bridges are quietly impressive too; they unite, bind communities together. Langwathby's bailey bridge, a 'temporary' structure to replace the sandstone one washed away in the floods of 1968 is still there, still carrying traffic – they'll get round to a new one some day and in 1700 a bridge was built between Ainstable and Armathwaite, the river being one of those neat, natural parish boundaries. The Church imposed different boundaries once, but the two riverside communities, inextricably historically linked, resisted and had them redrawn. Eventually. The river exerts an irresistible pull.

It is a solid structure, that bridge at Armathwaite; its early twentieth century improvements a post-industrial revolution triumphal flourish and in sharp contrast to the romanticism of Wordsworth's beloved walks just a little up river, or so it seemed until last winter when the river turned rogue, went mad and embarked on a violent spree of unprecedented destruction. Then, standing on the bridge with a frenzied torrent raging through its four arches, everything felt strangely fragile and vulnerable. Such a sudden unleashing of elemental might quickly rearranges any perceptions of human invincibility, puts us back in our place, reminds us that even in a mouse-clicking, techno-savvy, space-age world, there are some things quite beyond our control. Yes, we can build bridges and barns, we can plough fields, we can tinker around the edges, but nothing changes the brooding Pennine giants slumbering on the skyline or the gorge and the river beneath.

Living near the river is one thing; being near a bridge is another, especially as the bridges that cross the Eden are relatively few and scattered. It's about logistics, convenience, accessibility, yet people managed, got about, travelled in the past. Mary who lived at Rowfoot long before us, would drive her pony and trap laden with meats to Carlisle, eschewing Armathwaite bridge and using the ford at Holmwrangle to cross the river as it shortened the distance considerably. And quite suddenly, I am struck by just how very, very different the history, economy – the very life – of this valley would have been had the river been navigable.

Apart from an occasional fisherman's rowing boat, the only traffic on the Eden is a fleet of canoes, flying the rapids above Armathwaite Castle. It is a leisure paradise now; riders, cyclists and walkers use the paths and tracks that our predecessors used to go to Church or Chapel, or between farms.

Often, I walk by the mighty, roaring Eden, the placid, tranquil Eden, the dancing, peeping, leaping, sly and foxy now-I'm-here-now-I'm-not Eden and every time it is different: gaudy daffodils march ahead of me in Spring; all Summer my path is a tunnel of luscious green; in Autumn I saunter along gilded leaf-strewn paths beneath a bronzed canopy. In Winter an unfriendly chill bites at my hands and nips at my cheeks but come Spring again, we're on better terms, my river and I, as the woodland fills with flowers and sun glances through fresh foliage.

Paths converge, stray and merge, where the glade unfolds into woodland. Climb knotted tangles of tree roots and at the top of the hill beyond where the path widens out to the right, stands the one solid and unchanging constant, give or take a spangling of light or a falling shadow on the pink sandstone: the benchmark sculpture Vista. One of ten seats scattered the length of the Eden, these are seats for contemplation, reflection, seats where you can lose yourself entirely, immersed in Nature's extravagance. Vista is no Long Meg, Castlerigg nor ancient henge but a stone circle for our times. Hewn from the stone, trainers, a rucksack, a T-shirt and a towel speak of temporary abandonment; smaller satellite stones cluster round, waiting, waiting... lichen cling to Vista now, mellowing its rawness, reclaiming it as part of its native landscape. And just like me, Vista overlooks the great snaking loop of the Eden Gorge in wonder that this wild and extraordinary place contrives to be different every time, yet reassuringly the same.

Contradictory? Awe-inspiring? Mysterious? Yes, all those and more: intoxicating Eden still holds me in thrall.

Jackie Moffat

Felican Beck

The fish that lately left this stream
and from this silent brook retired:
knows it that like the sunny beam
its sight the lively thought inspired?

Know it that in this peaceful rill?
(where late it glided for a day)
no anglers come with guileful skill
to bait and hook and then betray?

Had fate indulgent fixed it here,
(for fishes may have fates that guide)
then had it shunned that smart severe,
which hooks may give the leften side.

For now it skims in Eden's flood
or laves it in the Cawdagan wave!
And there the fish are known so good
that nets or lines the youths all have.

Glide back then glide to this safe rill
to friendships current round this heart,
where drops no barbed hooks that kill,
nor in this stream is felt one smart.

For anglers round this heart ne'er throws
the waving line of feather'd flies,
nor with fond expectation glows
to catch the fishes as they rise.

Glide back my fish then glide away,
and safely swim from fishers free;
happy I'll spend each shorten'd day
when my dear fish shall skim by me.

Susanna Blamire

The Golden Triangle

My first response was disbelief. No one had ever told me that there was a remarkably beautiful bit of Cumbria that hadn't a single tea shop, not even a hint of a craft shop, not one tourist information kiosk, no roads wide enough to drive a coach up and therefore hardly any visitors.

It was the autumn of 1987 and we had just moved to Carlisle from Cleator Moor, with the vague intention of moving back south, probably to London. Then one day we took a drive out to Brampton and from there headed for the handsome little village of Walton, which might be described as one of the starting points of the Debatable Lands (the other starting point is the much higher profiled Lanercost). I had never even heard of Walton. Suddenly, just opposite its landmark spired church, I noticed a profusion of old handpainted Cumberland County Council signposts saying Solmain, Kirkcambeck, Roadhead and Bewcastle.

Those names seemed unusually affecting and exciting ones to me. I had vaguely heard of the last two, and in my ignorance assumed they were somewhere in Northumbria. So we followed our noses and drove up the principal highway of the North East Cumbrian uplands, the narrow and tortuous B6318 that starts way back in Greenhead, Northumbria and winds and unwinds all the way to Langholm. En route it takes in the backbone of the ancient Debatable Lands, which is both reiver country and Roman country and it also takes in some of the loveliest and most original landscape in the world.

I think it was when we first left the junction at Nickie's Hill and came down on the Wheatsheaf pub at Kirkcambeck that we realised we were on the road to somewhere absolutely extraordinary. Tiny Kirkcambeck by the way is pronounced 'Cammock' and there were once important animal auctions held here. Sad to say the locals not pronouncing the 'Kirk' bit was prophetic, now that the the gaunt but endearing old church up on the mound beside the Stapleton road has closed; when I spoke to the Lanercost minister who took monthly services there back in 1999 he told me the congregation varied between one and none. The pub likewise has gone which is a shame as the proprietors' sheepdog was a genius at catching beer mats and few things are more satisfying than throwing beermats for a young collie in a quiet country pub. Back in 1994 I once did location shooting there for a documentary about my novel Radio Activity (we were pretending that the Wheatsheaf was the Biggest Liar in the World pub at Santon Bridge) but that's another story.

The golden triangle of the Debatable Lands is that vast area of scattered smallholdings between Brampton, Longtown and the Roxburgh border just below Newcastleton. It has that closed kingdom feel to it that I associate with places like the Hebrides and for similar reasons. Up on the Isle of Coll a single farmstead will be called a 'township' and likewise almost every farm in North East Cumbria is called Somethingtown. There are road and footpath signs to Oldtown, Whamtown, Selbystown, Justicetown, Noblestown, all of them very old and handsome smallholdings. They might all have tiny populations but there is an amazing lattice of interconnecting C roads that join up the major farming areas of Bailey, Bewcastle, Roweltown, Penton and Easton. A great many of these C roads have no signpost and you need to know where you are going or you might never get out of the mazelike network.

Bafflingly within each principal hamlet there are sub-hamlets that occasionally function as major hamlets and generic areas within their own right. No one has ever managed to explain to me where the Roweltown sub-area of Stapleton (church and village hall) finishes and where Roweltown, which boasts the post office and sorting office, starts. And I still wonder why there is a prominent road sign to Oldtown which turns out to be a single farm.

It gets far tougher to interpret these demarcations when you get up to the windy fastnesses of Penton on the border. Bear with me as I try to explain Penton to you. It has at least five parts to it, most of them on average at least a mile from any other. Where the post office was you find a prosperous hamlet with the wonderful name of Catlowdy. Down from there is Penton Linns which is smack on the Scottish border next to Harelaw. The former railway station, once a great place for loading and unloading animal stock, might just be Penton proper, assuming such a thing could be said to exist. A mile on is the church which is called Nicholforest (referred to as The Nickle Forest in Walter Scott's Redgauntlet) and adjacent is the Kingfield pheasant rearing estate.

Just down from there was where Cumbria's smallest primary school last flourished in the 1980s. It was called Warwicksland which is also a sub-area of Penton. Proceed two miles further on and you are still in Penton but it is now called Bushfield, and is a clump of rugged forestry houses. Drive back about another four miles and you are half way between Penton and Easton. Somewhere around the defiantly named smallholding of Scuggate, the former finishes and the latter might tentatively claim to start. Yet look on many a road map and not one of these places can be found, but instead there is a place called Nook which is in fact a single Penton farm. Simple or what?

If this indeterminate geography sounds a little abstruse then you need to reflect that Penton / Nicholforest / Warwicksland / Nook / Bushfield / Catlowdy is in the very heartland of the Debatable Lands where lines, borders and exact demarcations literally meant life and death in the vicious old reiver days. Nowadays of course the only one-to-one fighting you'll see is the Cumberland Wrestling at Bewcastle Show, and the only large scale battles are bag whist drives at Roadhead Village Hall.

A final word about Roadhead, the forbidding but magnificent capital of the Golden Triangle. It is perched there in the middle of nowhere with the Solway Firth and the Roweltown and Bewcastle smallholdings glittering below it on a sunny day. In the Scots direction lies the austere beauty of the Bailey hills and the mystery that is Penton. The village is very long, very stark and bare in the winter, and the road through it has a sharp rectangular bend at either end. The signposts say things like Kinkry Hill and Dodgsonstown Ford, and nearby there are farms called Snouts and Dirtup.

Suffice to say you are not in Hampstead, but then neither are you in reassuring Ambleside or easy-on-the-eye Keswick. In 1987 Roadhead had a garage, a police station, a shop, and not a single dwelling was out of keeping with the sombre north east uplands surrounding. These days it has no shop, no garage, no policeman, but has two very smart housing estates that do their best to blend, but somehow would belong much better in Cockermouth or Windermere.

As a west Cumbrian who has chosen north east Cumbria as his adopted homeland, can I make a heartfelt plea that these developments happen somewhere else and we keep this remarkable area as it ought to be preserved?

John Murray

Flowers

For Winifred Nicholson

Flowers,
a dozen or more,
I picked one summer afternoon
from field and hedgerow.
Resting against a wall
I held them up
to hide the sun.
Cell by cell,
exact as dance,
I saw the colour,
structure, purpose
of each flower.
I named with their secret names.
They flamed in air.

But, waking
I remember only two
-soapwort and figwort,
the lilac and the brown.
The rest I guess at
but cannot see
-only myself,
almost a ghost upon the road,
without accoutrement,
holding the flowers
as torch and talisman
against the coming dark.

Frances Horovitz

The road

The road runs straight, like Hadrian's wall
nearby. Out in the wind, between coast
and coast, high nomansland, spectacular
wide-lidded skies, the sun's eye
balancing on cars. What blows through
is placenessness, the mother-stuff
you couldn't live with. Immanence
is all to do again, whether the heel-stamp
of a Roman god, or mocking waves
from jiggly severed hands in lorry-cabs.

William Scammell

Culvert

Stone stepping over,
cushioning arch
of cut and canted
stones, road's instep
riding the dip

of older workings
with the grain of the rock,
weatherings underground,
where water tells
another story

at cross-purposes
to this: bright threads
under memory, that pool
in memory's loss. Here
is a Roman thread,

a forethought of stone.

Roger Garfitt

An extract from The Bridal of Triermain

V1
'Then come thou hither, Henry, my page
whom I saved from the sack of Hermitage,
when that dark castle, tower and spire,
rose to the skies a pile of fire,
and redden'd all the Nine-stane Hill,
and the shrieks of death that wildly broke
through devouring flame and smothering smoke,
made the warrior's heart-blood chill.
The trustiest thou of all my train,
my fleetest courser thou must rein,
and ride to Lyulph's tower,
and from the baron of Triermain
greet well that sage of power.
He is sprung from Druid sires,
and British bards that tuned their lyres
to Arthur's and Pendragon's praise
and his who sleeps at Dunmailraise.
Gifted like his gifted race
he the characters can trace,
graven deep in elder time
upon Helvellyn's cliffs sublime;
sign and sigil well doth he know,
and can bode of weal and woe'
of kingdoms' fall, and fate of wars,
from mystic dreams and course of stars
he shall tell if middle earth
to that enchanting shape gave birth,
or if 'twas but an airy thing,
such as fantastic slumbers bring,
fram'd from the rainbow's varying dyes
or fading tints of western skies.
For, by the Blessed Rood I swear,
if that fair form breathe vital air,

no other maiden by my side
shall ever rest De Vaux's bride!

V11
The faithful Page he mounts his steed,
and soon he cross'd green Irthing's mead,
dash'd o'er Kirkoswald's verdant plain
and Eden barr'd his course in vain,
he passed red Penrith's Table Round,
for feats of chivalry renown'd,
left Mayburgh's mound and stones of power,
by Druids raised in magic hour,
and traced the Eamont's winding way,
till Ulfo's lake beneath him lay.

Walter Scott

He went down to the weir this morning

He went down to the weir this morning,
his elbows brushing through the old man's beard,
and on top of the arc the summer's rubbish
was caught -a single shoe, white sole,
canvas upper, and a fencepost on the cusp
of falling water- waiting for the first
autumn storm to take them. The river
is bright and icy now, still glints like chrome
beneath a pale dome of sky. Muscovy ducks
sit on stones. Butterflies, autumn burnished, are blown
like fallen leaves. A new term beckons.
New challenges, new chores. And at their finish,
when nights have drawn in and the tv chatters its trash,
he pictures himself staring at the vodka bottle
and tries to laugh at the absurdity
of a word like alone. A single tiny glint
of fish skitters, blind and furious against
the current, while behind the roar of water
a half heard whisper of rain
falls on the bristling upturned faces
of the fields like an answered prayer.

Nick Pemberton

The Kingdom of Sediment

1

Rust seemed to bleed downstream
from dumped washing tubs and pram wheels,
the way sheep leaked poison
as they lay dead at the source,
the taste sharp as smashed glass
if you cupped hands and sipped.

Our stream smelled of pennies sweating in a fist
and ran out from behind houses
into farmland. There, we mud-pied cows,
safe on one side as the herd wobbled, shy
at the water's edge, engrossed
in its broken reflection.

Sometimes we found a door
in a field. We'd shunt it into the stream,
then follow with branches, poking it sideways,
hoping it wouldn't wedge between banks:
when it stuck, we'd dare each other to step on,
though I was sure it would swing open

under me, as doors did when I leant against them
listening in, and pitch me through to the kingdom
of sediment, where leeches bled your shins
and bicycle spokes and ragged tins
slit the balls of your feet to the bone.

11

To the sewage works at the edge of town
I was led and drowned
while my brother kicked pebbles at a can,
furious when his shots flew wide and swam
under the slurry, breaking out trapped gas
as they were sucked down.

I was drawn by sticklebacks, through overflow pipes,
picking up the accent of the current
as I babbled down arterial byways:
I found my new tongue
could run around anything.

As the youngest under
I ascended to the throne,
ruling suicides and sea-fisherman
who've stolen into fresh water
to escape the gaping spaces of the ocean.

Sometimes I caress familiar ankles.
I hold them as the feet paddle,
but my hands shatter when they climb back out;
I feel heat beneath the skin,
and long to break the surface.

My sceptre was cast from flakes of iron
and mercury, siphoned from a salmon's gills;
my robes are trimmed with white-water,
my crown inlaid with bubbles, caught
while they still held flawless pearls of breath.

My orb is a kingfisher's egg
that rolled into the water as it hatched.
The fledgling peers from the crack
or lifts half its shell and shows me wings,
sodden at its sides. It knows no grief.
I tell it stories about above.

Jacob Polley

Casson Dyke

When the life of the city
has drained you from cuts,
at the uttermost point of defeat,
put on your motley,
come here as a penitent,
a pilgrim.

Come on foot
or an old fashioned bike,
you need not walk on your knees,
test yourself up the hill to Beaumont
and out to the flat plain beyond.
Go on 'til you reach the corner of land
then stop at the river
where she dies and becomes tide.

Take the place of the heron
stand small at the rim of the world's plate
in the stripe of light under a flat sky
where driftwood is stranded like seals.
Swans and seagulls have formed a band,
farm sound drifts in all directions.

Or come by water
slip into her with the Caldew
and make your way
down through the acid layers
to the hollow of her bed
scoured away by cutting.
Let her take you meandering
the long way round
as she lowers her banks
and spreads her green fringed skirts,
past red Rockcliffe on the right bank,
wade out over shore mud on the left.

Or come with the geese
in over Glasson Moss
where the sunken forest
lies in its grey airless tomb of clay;
past the ghostly camp of Edward's men
waiting to cross over
and fight the Scots again
or carry his body back home.
Sail on over farms, then come to land.

It is a place of edges
its power is strongest at the cusp.
Choose your moment carefully;
dawn, the longest day,
dusk, the shortest,
new moon.

At the exact place where all things should meet;
the countries borders
salt water and fresh,
air and earth,
sky and land,
a space will open clearly to you.
Do not stop to think
but follow your animal heart into the emptiness
like the Atlantic salmon
who flashes through transitional waters
up and up.

Here, where the river is spent
you will find a source of renewal.
Hope will flow.

Annie Foster

Back End

Another summer we must have blinked and missed,
as iron enters the soul of dews,
and trees announce their redundancies,
as the first leaves shuffle, disconsolate in doorways.

The crack swirls, as thick and familiar
as the leaves, or betting shop smoke:
A poor year, aye, nae doot aboot that:
there's nivver been twa good days togither.
And if all are agreed things aren't what they were,
they stopped looking for reasons in June.
Resignation's sunk in – the old candidates for blame,
say Concorde, and all them Russian missiles:
Weather's nut been t'shem since they went ta t' moon.
Have now (just about) been forgotten.
Some raise hopes still: *We'd a good September last year,*
and it's been nice down South and all,
though really, their thoughts are edging to Spain,
or to Christmas - next year could be better…

Yes there's always next year…
                                   For however clapped out,
wings rusted, shot gaskets, this once-good earth can seem,
we cling to the thought it can be patched up,
of renewal – which could keep us sane.
It's as if it were drawn at the top of our slates,
to plot out the framework, with space and time,
not subsistent, but a form of perception,
or deep structure, hard-wired in our tales
of Persephone's release, the Resurrection,
Barbarossa and Arthur, asleep in their caves,
till the call comes to make their countries whole.

And perhaps it's too lulling – shops rise up, neon-bright
from the braziers and rubble,
while grass grows to shrubs, and shrubs to trees
in kestrel-patrolled motorway cuttings.
When last year's quarries turn to nature reserves,
finality becomes hard to credit,
while we keep on hoping it will all work out,
all be given back somehow.
·- With biographies too – the Great Man's death
becomes as hard to believe in as our own,
on last chapters half-thinking, he might yet be alive,
if Beethoven only had had better doctors;
if only Wordsworth hadn't caught that chill…

If only we hadn't cut the rainforests down;
hadn't slaughtered all the whales…

Peter Rafferty

Sources and Acknowledgements

Susanna Blamire
Born in 1747 at Cardew Hall near Dalston, Susanna Blamire was brought up at Thackwood. She lived a quiet life but was much acclaimed for her poems, many of which were set to music. She died in 1794. The poem Felican Beck was dedicated to her dearest friend Elizabeth Beckwith Fisher and is set in the charmingly pastoral and deeply eroded miniature valley of the Fellican Beck, which flows past Thackwood, before descending in serpentine bends to the river Roe, a tributary of the River Caldew.

David Craig
Born in Aberdeen, David Craig lives in south Cumbria and for many years taught creative writing at Lancaster University. He has written several volumes of prose and poetry and Faces in the Rock is an extract taken from his book Landmarks, an exploration of great rocks around the world from his perspective as a climber. It is reproduced with the kind permission of the author. Copyright David Craig.

Josephine Dickinson
Born in London, Josephine Dickinson read Classics at Oxford and composed and taught music for many years. She has lived near Alston for more than a decade and has published three collections of her poems; Scarberry Hill, The Voice, and Silence Fell. The literary magazine Staple voted her one of the best poets of her generation. The poem Spells of the Raven was first commissioned by ECCP for the Cumbria Life magazine supplement Eden – An Accessible Paradise. Copyright Josephine Dickinson

Roger Deakin

Writer, film maker and a founding trustee of Common Ground, Roger Deakin was born in 1943 and completed his last book Wildwood: A Journey Through Trees just before he died in 2006.Descent into Hell Gill is taken from his book Waterlog (a swimmers journey through Britain) first published in 1999 by Chatto and Windus. Copyright belongs to The Random House Group Ltd.

Michael Ffinch

Michael Ffinch died in 1999. He lived for many years in the Ravenstonedale area and was well known as a poet, teacher, librettist, biographer and broadcaster. The poem Ravenstonedale Park is from his Selected Poems published in 1979 by Titus Wilson and Son Ltd. It is reproduced with the kind permission of his family.

Roy Fisher

Born in Birmingham, Roy Fisher is a poet and jazz pianist who now lives in Derbyshire. He was for many years a senior lecturer at the University of Keele and is the author of over thirty collections of poetry. His poem The Running Changes is from the collection The Long and the Short of it: poems 1955-2005, published by Bloodaxe Books, 2005. Copyright Bloodaxe Books.

Annie Foster

Born in Newcastle, Annie Foster settled in Carlisle in 1980 after living for some years in London and Nottingham. She was encouraged by Bill Scammell, who included her poems in his anthology The New Lake Poets published in 1991. She is a Quaker and is involved with Border Poets and Speakeasy who organise regular poetry readings in Carlisle. Her poem Casson Dyke was first commissioned by ECCP for the magazine supplement Eden – An Accessible Paradise. Copyright Annie Foster.

Roger Garfitt

Roger Garfitt lives in Shropshire and has been a full-time writer since he won the Gregory Award in 1974. He was once married to Frances Horovitz whose collected poems he edited in 1985. Culvert was written about an actual culvert under Hadrian's Wall at Gilsland and first appeared in Four Poets Four Artists published by YLC Press in 1981. Copyright Carcanet Press.

Jane Gardam

Jane Gardam won the The Heywood Hill Literary Prize for a Lifetime contribution to Literature, the Whitbread Fiction Award twice, one of which was for The Hollow Land, and was shortlisted for the Booker Prize for her novel God on the Rocks. The extract from Tomorrow's Arrangements is taken from her book The Hollow Land published by Puffin - copyright David Higham Associates Ltd.

Sarah Hall

Born in Cumbria, Sarah Hall lives in Carlisle and is a regular contributor to Cumbria Life magazine. Haweswater, her first novel, won the Commonwealth Writers Prize in 2003. Her second book, Electric Michelangelo was shortlisted for the Man Booker Prize in 2004 and she has just published her third novel The Carhullan Army. The extract from Haweswater is reproduced with the permission of the publisher Faber and Faber.

Pip Hall

Pip Hall lives in Dentdale and is a calligrapher who specializes in letter carving, mainly in stone. Best known for her work with Meg Peacocke on the poetry path at Kirkby Stephen, she is also a letter designer, print maker and illustrator. The illustrations in this book derive from the linoprints she made, which were used to produce the bronze panels on the Discover Eden walking routes. Pip Hall retains copyright for reproduction of these images.

Frances Horovitz

Poet, teacher, broadcaster and actor, Frances Horovitz died in 1983 aged 45 after a long illness. She spent the two years before her tragic death living near Birdoswald with her husband Roger Garfitt. Flowers was written at that time following her meeting with the painter Winifred Nicholson, who lived at Banks, and first appeared in the pamphlet Snow Light, Water Light which was a collection of all her Cumbrian poems edited by Roger Garfitt. It is reproduced with the kind permission of Bloodaxe Books.

Kathleen Jones

Kathleen Jones was born and bred on a hill farm in the Eden Valley. She is a poet and biographer whose books have included The Life of Christina Rossetti, Catherine Cookson; the Biography and A Passionate Sisterhood, which tells the story of the sisters, wives and daughters of the Lake poets. Reflections first appeared in the Cumbria Life magazine supplement Eden – An Accessible Paradise. Copyright Kathleen Jones.

Jackie Moffat

A regular contributor to Cumbria Life magazine with a column about life on her smallholding at Ainstable, Jackie Moffat is also the author of two books, The Funny Farm and Sheepwrecked. Her essay Voluptuous Eden was originally commissioned for the magazine Eden – An Accessible Paradise. Copyright Jackie Moffat.

John Murray

Born in West Cumbria, John Murray was educated at Oxford. He now lives near Brampton and has written five novels, to great critical acclaim, including Radio Activity, and Jazz etc. The Golden Triangle first appeared in the magazine Eden – An Accessible Paradise. Copyright John Murray.

Norman Nicholson

Author of six collections of poetry, Norman Nicholson lived in Cumbria most of his life and died in 1987. He received the Queens Gold Medal for Poetry in 1997. The poem Cockley Moor was written when he visited Helen Sutherland, a patron of the arts, at her home on the western slopes above Ullswater and was published in his Collected Poems by Faber and Faber. It is included in this anthology by permission of David Higham Associates.

Mick North

Mick North is the Arts Officer for Carlisle City Council. He is also a published poet and won the Gregory Award in 1986. His poem Shap was first published in his collection 'The Pheasant Pluckers Son' by Littlewood +Arc in 1990 - copyright Mick North.

Meg Peacocke

Meg Peacocke has published three critically acclaimed collections of her poems - Marginal Land, Selves, and Speaking of the Dead, all published by Peterloo Poets. She wrote the poems for the Poetry Path at Kirkby Stephen and is a winner of the prestigious Cholmondeley Award for distinction in poetry. Her poem The Shaping of Eden first appeared in the Cumbria Life Magazine supplement Eden, An Accessible Paradise. Copyright M.R. Peacocke.

Nick Pemberton

Born in Manchester, Nick Pemberton has lived in Cumbria close to the river Eden for over thirty years. He is head of Creative Writing at the University of Cumbria. The poem He went Down to the Weir This Morning is reproduced with permission of the author.

Tom Pickard

Newcastle born Tom Pickard lives high up on the Pennines. He has published numerous collections of poetry including Hole in the Wall: New and Selected Poems and The Dark Months of May, published by Flood editions. The poem Below the Ridge is from his collection Ballad of Jamie Allan published in 2007 by Flood Editions, Chicago. Copyright Tom Pickard.

Jacob Polley

Born in Carlisle, Jacob Polley's first book of poems, The Brink, was a Poetry Book Society Choice and was short-listed for five awards. He was selected as one of the Next Generation group of up and coming new poets in 2004 and appointed Visiting Fellow Commoner in the Creative Arts 2005 - 2007 at Trinity College, Cambridge. He published his second collection, Little Gods, in 2006. His poem The Kingdom of Sediment is from 'The Brink' published by Pan Macmillan 2003. Copyright Pan Macmillan.

Peter Rafferty

Born in Carlise, Peter Rafferty still lives in the city where he is the manager of a betting shop. He studied Geography at Manchester, Geomorphology at Durham and is a Italophile, wine expert and poet. A collection of his poems, entitled Eoliths, was published by Arrowhead Press in 2002. The poem Back End is reproduced with permission of the author.

Kathleen Raine

Kathleen Raine died in 2003. She was the author of eleven books of poetry and four volumes of autobiography. She was a founder of the Temenos Academy of Integral Studies and editor of the Temenos Review. She was awarded the Queens Gold Medal for Poetry in 1992 and made a CBE in 2000. Her poem The River is printed by permission of The Estate of Kathleen Raine from The Collected Works of Kathleen Raine (Golgonooza Press, 2000) Copyright Kathleen Raine 2000.

William Scammell

William Scammell published nine books of poetry and several anthologies between 1979 and 1998. He received a Cholmondeley Award in 1980. He was working on a series of new poems when he died in 2000 aged 61. These were published by Flambard Press two years later in the collection Black and White. His poem The Road is printed here by kind permission of his widow, Jan Scammell.

Walter Scott

Born in Edinburgh in 1771, Walter Scott spent his early years in the Scottish / English borders which were to have such a profound effect on his writing. Initially known as a poet, he refused the offer of poet laureate in 1813 to concentrate on the historical novels for which he is most famous including Waverly, Rob Roy and Ivanhoe. He died in 1832.

William Wordsworth

Wordsworth spent much of his childhood in Penrith and, although in adulthood he lived most of his life in the central Lake District, he continued to make occasional forays eastward. The lake in his famous poem Daffodils is, of course, Ullswater, very much part of the Eden catchment. While the Poor Gather Round relates to the Countess' Pillar which is situated just east of Brougham Castle. It was erected by Lady Anne Clifford in memory of her mother and for the annual distribution of money to the poor of the parish.

An accessible paradise

'Discover Eden' is about forging a deeper engagement with the unique territorial chemistry that defines Eden and there is no better way to explore the landscape than walking on public footpaths, bridleways and byways. The Public Rights of Way network is a vital resource for exploring the countryside. It allows us to inhabit rural landscapes more intimately, facilitating access to both natural and human heritage sites which might otherwise not be available to us.

Most public paths have existed for centuries and enable us, quite literally, to follow in the footsteps of our predecessors from the earliest Bronze Age tribespeople, Roman soldiers and cattle drovers, to postmen in more recent times delivering mail on foot to every farm, and children walking, through fields and woods, to and from school.

Nature too has benefited over the years as many public paths, particularly when they are contained by hedges and walls, have become havens for a wide variety of wildlife, safe from harmful agricultural activity, and provide us with miles of linear nature reserves criss-crossing the countryside.

East Cumbria Countryside Project has devised a series of fourteen circuital routes on Public Rights of Way dispersed around the whole Eden catchment. All the routes have been improved so that they facilitate easier access and are clearly way-marked with arrows and the distinctive 'Discover Eden' kingfisher logo.

You will also find Pip Hall's linoprint images, etched into small bronze panels and attached to posts, at intervals along each route. The images depict aspects of human and natural heritage and rubbings can be taken from them using paper and crayons. There are six along each route, so by walking all fourteen routes you can eventually collect eighty four images.

Full colour interpretative guide booklets are available for each route to enhance your enjoyment and there is also a rubbings pack to help you collect those images.

For further information contact
    East Cumbria Countryside Project
    telephone 01228 564840
    email eccp@carlisle.gov.uk
    website www.eccp.org.uk

Lino prints for bronze motifs
from the 'Discover Eden' walk routes